THE UNSPOKEN TRUTH ABOUT GLOBALIZATION

THE UNSPOKEN TRUTH ABOUT GLOBALIZATION

◆

Eight Essays

Peter E. Temu

iUniverse, Inc.
New York Lincoln Shanghai

THE UNSPOKEN TRUTH ABOUT GLOBALIZATION
Eight Essays

iUniverse books may be ordered through booksellers or by contacting:

iUniverse
2021 Pine Lake Road, Suite 100
Lincoln, NE 68512
www.iuniverse.com
1-800-Authors (1-800-288-4677)

The views expressed in this work are solely those of the author and do not necessarily reflect the views of the publisher, and the publisher hereby disclaims any responsibility for them.

ISBN: 978-0-595-43379-7 (pbk)

ISBN: 978-0-595-87705-8 (ebk)

Printed in the United States of America

Contents

The 'UNSPOKEN TRUTH' Series of Booklets GENERAL
FOREWORD TO THE SERIES vii

INTRODUCTION 1

Essay # 1 WHAT IS GLOBALIZATION? 3

Essay # 2 'GOOD' AND 'BAD' GLOBALIZATION 5

Essay # 3 GLOBALIZATION AND LIBERALIZATION 8

Essay # 4 THE GLOBALIZATION OF POVERTY 13

Essay # 5 GLOBALIZATION AND THE EROSION OF
NATIONAL SOVEREIGNTY 21

Essay # 6 'INTELLECTUAL PROPERTY' AS A BARRIER TO
'GOOD' GLOBALIZATION 25

Essay # 7 GLOBALIZATION'S HIDDEN AGENDA: A
CHALLENGE TO AMERICA'S LEADERSHIP 30

Essay # 8 TOWARDS BALANCED GLOBALIZATION: A ROLE
FOR THE UNITED NATIONS 37

ABOUT THE AUTHOR 41

SUGGESTED READING 43

The 'UNSPOKEN TRUTH'
Series of Booklets
GENERAL FOREWORD TO THE SERIES

By
Peter E. Temu

The Unspoken Truth booklets, to which this publication belongs, is a series of essays written in the full knowledge that they will be controversial. Big business, multilateral donors and dominant groups in society, to say nothing of governments, will find that the hidden truth exposed in these essays runs counter to their interests.

This series of booklets exposes the campaign of hypocrisy by vested interests which the world has tolerated for far too long. It is a campaign that relies on theories which have long been discredited and yet are deliberately invoked to prey on people whose poverty, fear and ignorance often prevent them from seeing the picture in its full perspective.

The Unspoken Truth booklets are not research monographs, unveiling new truths. They are merely bold re-statements of certain home truths, to which theory, experience, common sense and empirical findings bear ample testimony. But these truths are unpopular and are often glossed over because they run counter to powerful vested interests.

INTRODUCTION

This presentation is in the form of eight short essays. Essay # 1 discusses the meaning of globalization. It alerts the reader to the fact that the literature on globalization must be read guardedly, since the term is sometimes used extremely loosely. Casual remarks about globalization tend to obscure more than they reveal.

Essay # 2 distinguishes between 'good' and 'bad' globalization. The definitions are normative, but operationally useful. Globalization is good and worth supporting if its impact on world development is balanced, or equitable; if it does not benefit some people, or some countries, at the expense of others. In the opposite case, globalization is bad, or detrimental.

Essay # 3 discusses two closely related phenomena, namely, globalization and liberalization. Both hold equal sway in contemporary academic and policy circles. The section reveals the intricate way in which the two processes are inter-twined.

Essay # 4 discusses the 'globalization of poverty', a deliberately provocative theme which is the title of an entire book by Michel Chossudovsky The detrimental impact of the IMF/World Bank reforms is well brought out in his brilliant masterpiece.

Essay # 5 shows how globalization, if unchecked, can seriously jeopardize national sovereignty.

Essay # 6 explains why 'intellectual property'—a euphemism for knowledge monopoly—is inimical to 'good' globalization.

Essay # 7 is essentially an attack on the use of double standards by vested interests in the developed countries which do not practice in their own countries what they preach to the rest of the world. The challenge to America's leadership—which that country has yet to confront—is to rise above the hidden agenda of selfish national interests and pursue the higher and nobler, if more difficult, goal of global equity.

Essay # 8 discusses globalization operating under an agreed code of conduct, designed to promote equitable global development. The author believes that the United Nations, for all its shortcomings, is still the nearest thing to World Government and, *if suitably reformed*, could both formulate and enforce the ground rules necessary for good globalization—the kind that would be beneficial to humanity as a whole. Such ground rules should be binding both on governments and on Transnational Corporations. Herein lies the challenge to American leadership of the world in the post-Cold War era.

Essay # 1
WHAT IS GLOBALIZATION?

An otherwise useful expression, *globalization* is in danger of becoming a meaningless cliché. Reportedly, the term was first used by Theodre Levitt in his book *The Globalization of Markets* published in 1985. Barely three years later, in 1988, Panic was already observing that the term has now come into such common usage—used and misused by economists, politicians, journalists, international bureaucrats and technocrats—that it has become a debased coin. It is used, and confused, with terms like 'openness', 'independence', and 'integration' (of different national economies into a single world economy) which are somewhat different concepts and involve many other factors and elements.

Our first aim is to see what light, if any, the concept of globalization can shed on our understanding of the nature, and hopefully the solution, of development problems in the world in general, and the Third World in particular, at the dawn of the new millenium. Our second aim is to study the challenge that globalization poses to America's leadership of the world in its current capacity as the sole superpower in the post-Cold War era.

The dictionary defines globalization as "the act, process, or policy of making something worldwide in scope and application". One point is clearly implicit in this definition, namely, that globalization is a process *engineered by man*. It is part of the international economic and social environment which, in the words of Mwalimu Julius Nyerere, is not God-given, but man-made, and those who design it and run it are the powerful from the North.

The concept of globalization is not, and cannot be, confined to economics or indeed to any single discipline. As a phenomenon which impacts human society in many different ways, globalization is essentially multidimensional, and is therefore a relevant subject of study for various academic disciplines.

Any meaningful discussion of the subject must avoid using the term 'globalization' in a way that confuses the process with its end-result. The discussion should also pinpoint, from the start, exactly what it is that is being, or has been, globalized. Only then can one talk sensibly about the pros and cons of globalization, its value and limitations, its merits and demerits.

One observer likens globalization to a runaway train, an "out of control money making system that is eating up both the earth and human communities". Another sees it as a force that is charging "at break-neck speed without map or compass" Yet, we cannot but reject the notion that globalization is an all-powerful autonomous monster that man can do nothing about. We need to explode the *myth* that "economic globalization is a natural phenomenon like continental drift: impossible to resist or control", and acknowledge the *truth* that "in reality, globalization is being shaped and advanced by carefully planned legal and institutional changes embodied in a series of international agreements"

It would seem, then, that globalization is neither natural nor inevitable: it is simply a process engineered by those who have a vested interest in its outcome. To the extent that society considers it desirable to do so, the process can be controlled or even reversed. This will not happen automatically or easily, because of resistance by powerful vested interests. It is therefore necessary to study the nature of the globalization process, assess its impact, understand who benefits and who loses from it, and then try to live up to the challenge that it poses.

Essay # 2
'GOOD' AND 'BAD' GLOBALIZATION

The reason why there is so much confusion about globalization is because the term means different things to different people. If globalization simply means 'going global', the term can indeed be applied to just about anything.

To be a meaningful concept, free from ambiguity, globalization needs a rigorous operational definition, one that is acceptable—or at least understandable—to its users. The first step towards such a definition is to understand clearly what it is that is being globalized. Anytime the subject comes up for discussion, one must hasten to ask, from the outset—"globalization of *what?*"

In the popular literature it is possible, if not common, to talk of the globalization of trade, finance, communications, manufacturing, technology, etc.; equally well, one may talk of the globalization of poverty, pollution, or even crime. Our own interest is in the globalization of *development*. Other aspects of globalization are studied with that end in view. An attempt is made to analyze those global forces or undercurrents which are conducive to accelerated global development, and therefore inimical to global poverty. The focus of the presentation is how to spearhead world development, using the instrumentality of various underlying global forces. Ideally, the objective is the attainment of *balanced* globalization, or balanced world development. Such globalization may be viewed as 'good', or socially desirable, in contrast to the growing marginalization of the developing countries that typically characterizes 'bad' globalization trends.

We must not be hung up on semantics, either as to what constitutes development or balanced development. The time is long past when such questions would provoke heated academic debates. In today's information age, when endless TV broadcasts bring every corner of the world vividly to our living rooms, even a child knows, intuitively, the difference between rich and poor, and between extremes of wealth and poverty. The problem does not lie in our failure to understand, but merely in our failure—or refusal—to confront the challenge.

If balanced global development is our ultimate goal, then we must recognize that, left to itself, the process of globalization will not automatically bring it about; if anything, just the contrary. The world must take purposeful action to guide globalization along constructive channels. Such a task can only be entrusted to a <u>reformed</u> United Nations, not to giant transnational corporations or to so-called superpowers.

What this means is that positive global trends must be identified and fostered, while negative ones are suppressed. This calls for the adoption of correct policies by governments in the developed and developing countries alike, and the support and goodwill of the international community, including the transnational corporations.

Let us make one point perfectly clear. Correct policies as envisaged here are a far cry from the so-called 'sound' policies which are the hallmark of the Bretton Woods institutions—the International Monetary Fund and the World Bank—prescriptions. In the present context, correct policies are those which would encourage balanced or equitable globalization. By contrast, 'sound' policies *a la* Bretton Woods are precisely those which are fuelling the present type of runaway globalization, and continuing to widen the gap between the world's rich and poor.

Two points emerge. First, that it is important to be clear exactly what is being globalized; second, that it is just as important to understand *in whose interests* globalization is taking place. Our normative assumption is that balanced (or equitable) development, national as well as global, is the basic objective. Globalization is good if it furthers that objective, bad if it undermines it. Globalization is desirable if it is the kind that promotes the interests of humanity at large (which is what constitutes balanced or equitable development); and undesirable if it is the kind that helps entrench the vested interests of some groups of people, or of countries, at the expense of others.

We need hardly add that the 'globalization' of any criminal activity, such as drug trafficking, money laundering, computer-virus dissemination or, in general, the abuse of cyberspace technology, is bad in itself. Although it has been deliberately kept outside the scope of our discussion, such globalization must be recognized as an extremely powerful force *for evil,* which the world can only neglect at its peril.

Essay # 3
GLOBALIZATION AND LIBERALIZATION

In principle, globalization and liberalization go hand in hand. Liberalization is a necessary, but not a sufficient, condition for globalization. Liberalization consists in a set of laws and practices which permit resources (human, institutional and financial) to move freely across national boundaries and within the domestic market. Without liberalization, globalization would be virtually impossible. It is for this reason that the euphoria about globalization has the same root, and comes in the same train, as the euphoria about liberalization.

At the core of the globalization process are the transnational corporations (TNCs). Through the instrumentality of the WTO, the TNCs now seek 'the right to establish operations in any country they want, buy whatever they want, and repatriate as much profit as they want' This poses a serious threat to national sovereignty, and may rightly be regarded as part of the political price of globalization.

Balanced globalization—our normative objective—implies growth with equity across countries. It follows that there is need to examine critically if, and to what extent, globalization and its *sine qua non,* liberalization, are conducive to balanced world development. Invariably, the relevant question is, how far a given global trend tends to raise incomes, employment, and human welfare generally in the countries or regions which it impacts. Does the development impact benefit each country fairly, or does it benefit some countries more than (or at the expense of) others? In so far as the latter is the case, globalization causes global maldevelopment. Attractive and profitable as it may be to the TNCs themselves, or to the beneficiary countries, such globalization is undesirable from our standpoint and should be deplored. But to the extent that the benefits of globalization are more evenly spread, then globalization is a positive force for development, and deserves to be fostered and encouraged.

Though not always openly admitted, the drive or rationale for economic liberalization lies in the free market model. Free mobility of factors of production, the freedom of entry of new firms and exit of old firms, free trade without distortions due to taxes and subsidies, the free convertibility of currencies—these are the hallmark of the free market model, for centuries lauded by economists for its efficient allocation of resources and distribution of income. The process of liberalization entails the removal, where they exist, of such impediments as tariff and non-tariff barriers, exchange controls, prohibitions, licensing, immigration restrictions, work permits, etc.

By definition, government controls of any sort, intended to regulate the economy, interfere with the people's freedom of choice. The demolition of such controls—the removal of so-called market 'distortions'—is the essence of all liberalization policies. Liberalists argue that governments should only maintain law and order (plus basic infrastructure), leaving the people free to pursue their own economic interests. Indeed, classical *laissez-faire* theorists maintained that when an individual pursues his own selfish interests, he is guided "as if by an invisible hand" to pursue the interests of the community as a whole. This is liberalism *par excellence:* it rules out the need for any deliberate public intervention for the benefit of the community, whose welfare is supposedly best served when the individual's freedom of action is guaranteed.

Liberalization provides economic space, or a congenial environment, for the exercise of economic freedom, not only by individuals, but by corporations, large and small. The TNCs fit well into this picture. It remains to be seen whether the process of globalization, nurtured by liberalization, and spearheaded by the TNCs, helps or hinders world development.

A close look at the record reveals that liberalization is a mixed blessing. To begin with, the free market mechanism, which it is supposed to foster, barely exists. The rough and tumble of economic life in the real world paints a very different picture.

Moreover, it has long been realized that the analytical elegance of the free market model disappears the moment we abandon its simplistic, and patently absurd, underlying assumptions. These assumptions have been exhaustively discussed in the literature, and even the most ardent adherents of the free market model have been unable to defend them. Since these assumptions are the foundation of economic science, their outright denial would reduce economics to an empty shell. Many volumes have been written decrying the inadequacies of orthodox economics, and proposing an alternative economics. But all this effort seems to have been deliberately sidelined and treated as if it was just the voice of a few misguided dissidents. The truth is that orthodox economists, as a class, live in morbid fear of being declared redundant: the more the irrelevance of their subject is exposed, the more desperately they try to cling to their pet theories.

The reason why, almost in spite of itself, the orthodox free market theory continues to hold sway is because its conclusions are strongly supportive of, and cherished by, powerful vested interests. They also form the ideological underpinnings of Western capitalism and liberal democracy. For example, the notorious structural adjustment programmes (SAPs), which the World Bank and the IMF have been imposing uniformly on Third World countries as loan conditionalities, rest wholly on the theoretical pillars of the (otherwise discredited) free market model.

A couple of examples will suffice to demonstrate how outdated the orthodox model is. First, the model assumes that each firm within an industry is a price taker, that is, too small to influence the market; that there is perfect knowledge; and that firms can enter or leave the industry at will. This abstract scenario is a perfect setting for a liberal *laissez-faire* world economy. Yet, the picture is a far cry from the real world in which corporate giants dominate the planet. You have only to glance at *Fortune's 500* leading companies to see that there are many individual TNCs today which are many times larger than the economies of several countries put together. One could not possibly fit this scenario into the analytical framework of the orthodox model of 'atomistic' competition.

A second example relates to money and finance. Today, huge quantities of money flow back and forth across national boundaries at the push of a button, prompted by sheer economic speculation, and not because of any real international trade or investment transactions. These highly volatile movements of capital can, and do, make a far-reaching impact on the real economies of the countries concerned. Not only do the forces they generate negate the conclusions of the orthodox free market model, but they are often powerful enough to undermine the national sovereignty of governments.

More illustrative examples could be cited to show the irrelevance of the free market model and its conclusions, particularly if we bear in mind—as we should—not only what the model assumes, but what it assumes *away*. But there is no need to labour the point.

What is definitely irksome is the hypocritical use of double standards by those who purport to believe in the free market model and its prescriptions. These double standards are evident, for instance, in the selective targeting of the LDCs with respect to SAPs and liberalization. Market-based policies are fervently advocated as 'sound' or 'rational', and imposed on LDC governments by Western donors, using the coercive arm of the World Bank, the IMF, and the WTO. But no similar pressure is brought to bear (as both logic and fairness would have demanded) on the developed countries themselves to adopt the same policies. Unfortunately, this *asymmetry,* far from being accidental, is quite deliberate, and is manifested across the entire policy spectrum. Countries are simply not judged by the same yardstick.

Thus, discussions on wage and price rigidities, restrictions on labour mobility, protection of 'intellectual property', subsidies on agriculture, etc. always have a lob-sided bias in favour of the developed countries. Food or farm subsidies in the LDCs, for instance, are frowned upon and regarded as something that 'distorts' the efficient operation of the free market; whereas similar subsidies in the industrialized countries are viewed as perfectly legitimate 'safeguards' that enable farmers to stay in business.

Likewise, cheap labour from the LDCs is deliberately barred from entering developed countries so as not to depress wages, while cheap capital from the developed countries is supposed to enter the LDCs freely in the name of economic liberalization. Logically, liberalization demands, of course, that all countries *without exception* pull down barriers against the international mobility of labour, and of capital, in order to eliminate market distortions in any shape or form. There can be no double standards. Liberalization is either good for all or it is good for none.

Essay # 4
THE GLOBALIZATION OF POVERTY

Undoubtedly, there is something eerie, even repugnant, about the very expression 'globalization of poverty'. Globalizing poverty is surely the last thing anybody wants, and the last thing that those who sing the praises of globalization would like anyone to think about. Globalizing wealth, yes; globalizing poverty, no.

Yet, the 'globalization of poverty' is neither a contradiction in terms nor a cynical twist of reality. This theme is indeed the exact title of a thought-provoking book by Professor Michel Chossudovsky to whom this author is greatly indebted. As will be seen in the following pages, this expression dramatically draws attention *away* from the current euphoria about the imaginary virtues of globalization, towards its real danger, namely, the increased polarization of wealth and poverty that uncontrolled globalization brings in its train.

Significantly, the sub-title of Chossudovsky's book is *Impacts of World Bank and IMF Reforms*. The book is a brilliant critique of the manner in which the Bretton Woods institutions which style themselves agents of world development have, in fact, degenerated into vehicles of global impoverishment, and become the debt collectors for international creditors. According to the author, "The globalization of poverty in the late twentieth century is unprecedented in world history". For our purposes, the perpetuation of poverty, its global dissemination, and its aggravation through the policies of the Bretton Woods institutions, will be touched upon only briefly, with reference to external indebtedness, structural adjustment, and the liberalization policies which they impose on the

LDCs. The harmful effects of those policies and the shameless application of double standards by their perpetrators will be addressed elsewhere.

(i) Poverty and external indebtedness.

No economic evil greater than the external debt burden has ever befallen the developing countries. External indebtedness is the single most important factor that vitiates their development efforts—a problem which, if unsolved, could doom the developing countries to continue wriggling in their poverty, and eliminate any chance of their catching up with the industrialized countries. If you think this is overstated, just run a simple computer simulation in which you plug in realistic, even modest, values for the relevant variables, e.g. economic growth rates, current debt levels, debt servicing as percentage of export earnings, etc. You will find that the external debt is unpayable; that if present trends continue, the day may not be far off when a man in the developing countries will be spending his entire life working, not to raise his living standard, nor to educate his children, but merely to re-pay external creditors!

The blunt truth is that measures which are simply a short-run palliative of the debt, while perpetuating or adding to it in the long run, can never constitute a genuine solution to the debt problem. They merely entrench it and postpone the day of reckoning. The notorious debt re-schedulings *a la* Paris and London Clubs (resulting from the so-called 'Consultative Meetings' organized by the World Bank) offer no solution. All they do is to force one LDC after another to make concessions by submitting to humiliating conditions in order to maintain a semblance of financial credibility, which *temporarily* qualifies them for more loans, only to end up a few years later more steeped in debt than ever before.

The creditors, of course, know and anticipate this, and use any number of ingenious ways to sugar the pill. One of them is to 'forgive' a small portion of the debt, while extending new short-term credit on 'softer' terms; or they may throw in an occasional grant every now and then, with or without additional conditionalities. Be that as it may, the carefully pre-calculated end result is always the same: the debtor country ends up more indebted than before. To remain credit-worthy, it must again seek fresh quick-disbursing loans, and/or pray for further debt forgiveness. This leads to more Paris/London Club-type 'consultations'; more debt re-schedulings; etc. It is the same cycle all over again, only that each time the screws are a little bit tighter and things a little bit worse for the debtor country. Correspondingly, as can be seen from their increasingly patronizing rhetoric, the power and arrogance of the creditors mounts!

Is there any way out of this quandary, this debt trap? Personally, I do not believe that there is any simple escape from this state of permanent enslavement. One possibility—an extreme option—is debt repudiation. But the mere thought of it is enough to send shivers up the creditors' spines. Yet, while repudiation may not seem a serious option, for fear of the retaliatory consequences, it remains an option nevertheless. One scenario where repudiation (or a credible threat of it) *could* be effective is the case where all indebted countries agreed to stand firmly together and confront their creditors *en bloc*. Unfortunately, the extremely large number of debtor countries vying against each other virtually eliminates any chance of such concerted action, *to the absolute delight of the creditors.*

Furthermore, be it remembered that the creditors are well-seasoned, far-sighted, bureaucrats who take a long view. Despite their superior negotiating position, they do not just sit back to enjoy their comfortable advantage. Instead, they take purposeful action to ensure that the debtor countries do stay divided. It is precisely for this reason that at the Paris/London Clubs 'negotiations', creditors insist that debtor countries be dealt with one by one. This familiar 'divide and rule' tactic—an old lesson from colonialism—is cynically portrayed by the creditors as if it was a recognition on their part that each debtor country, being sovereign, deserved to be treated *on its own merits*. What flattery!

Imagine a poor, debt-distressed country, pitted against the world's most powerful and sophisticated multilateral creditors, led by the Bretton Woods giants! 'Negotiating' is just diplomatic language for 'taking dictation'. Their Excellencies never call a spade a spade. It is no secret that key government documents for the LDCs are sometimes drafted by World Bank/IMF officials in Washington D.C., and then sent to LDC ministers who dot the i's, cross the t's, Anglicise the spellings, affix their signatures, and then return them to Washington D.C. as their 'own' documents.

Debt repudiation—except as a last resort—must be ruled out as a viable option, because it is against international norms of good financial conduct. That leaves only one realistic option for debtor countries, namely, entering into *serious negotiations* with their creditors.

Let it be said at once that the Paris/London Club-style 'consultative meetings' are not negotiations in the true sense. Serious negotiation is a process in which all sides have a fair say, and any agreements reached are in the nature of a compromise which reflects the balance of 'give and take' by all parties.

Against this, I see the Paris and London forums as nothing more than places where LDC governments go to be dictated to, and made to submit to humiliating take-it-or-leave-it terms. It is something of a carrot-and-stick scenario. With little voice and even less clout, a debtor country is given a concession here and there, and promised this or that subsequent reward, *provided* that its performance meets the donors' criteria. Its policies are subjected to continuous surveillance, and the 'reform package' is closely monitored to ensure that its implementation does not fall behind schedule or otherwise deviate from the agreed path. The country is then given a stern warning as to the dire consequences that are bound to ensue should its government fail to behave exactly as it is told.

The Paris/London Club 'consultations' are therefore a far cry from the kind of serious negotiations that the situation calls for. To serve any useful purpose, Paris and London must adopt a more genuine negotiating posture. At present, the donor side has complete supremacy, which reduces to a mockery any idea of negotiated agreements. Consisting of the World Bank, the IMF and bilateral donors, the donor side is solid and impregnable—in fact, powerful *to the point of arrogance*. By contrast, the debtor side is the exact opposite—weak, ill-prepared, and virtually in disarray. Realistically, what the situation requires is solidarity on the part of the debtor countries, not in order to repudiate their debts (though this option must be kept open), or to beg for forgiveness, but in order to exert common leverage and bring their collective bargaining power to bear on the creditors.

(ii) The World Bank, the International Monetary Fund (IMF), and the globalization of poverty.

The World Bank and the IMF are a necessary evil: *evil* because they knowingly globalize poverty while pretending to globalize development; *necessary* because the world needs them to clean up the mess they have created. The dilemma they pose is both a bitter irony and a painful paradox.

The World Bank and the IMF know full well that their lob-sided policies protect the interests of the developed countries at the expense of the LDCs. This has put the LDCs on the horns of a dilemma: they detest the Bretton Woods giants for the harm they are doing to their economies, and yet they know that they need their assistance if they are ever to get out of the quagmire.

'World development' is the boastful title the World Bank sometimes gives to its annual reports. This is as deliberate a misnomer as is the self-styled *World* Bank itself. The institution's correct name is, of course, *The International Bank for Reconstruction and Development (IBRD)*. The IBRD was set up to rebuild Europe after its devastation in World War II. World development by any definition is not, and never has been, part of its mandate. Anyone who is prone to argue that the IBRD's original mandate has since changed to make global development its main focus must bear the burden of proof; his onus is not only to furnish statutory evidence but also to explain why the Bank should be going about it in exactly the wrong way. If world development were indeed its aim, why would the Bank be dealing with countries—or rather governments—piecemeal on an individual basis? Why should it almost never take cognizance of the manner in which policies designed for one country impinge upon the economic fortunes of another, or how the totality of its much-celebrated 'country programmes' affects world development as a whole?

A fatal flaw in the World Bank's approach to the solution of development problems is its notorious tendency—shared with the IMF—of prescribing the same standard solutions for the economic problems of every country. Indeed the policy menu is so uniform that it is nowadays called, sarcastically, the World Bank (or IMF) "medicine". This naïve one-size-fit-all formula is based on obsolete textbook theories and policy prescriptions of a freely competitive market economy, which ignore the stark realities of the practical world.

The sociologists' maxim—the 'fallacy of composition'—which maintains that the whole is larger than the sum of its parts, calls to mind one of these stark realities. Strangely, the World Bank and the IMF have chosen to ignore this elementary principle. They do not wish to recognize that the global economy is more than the sum of its parts, and that policies tailored to suit the economies of individual countries may, in their totality, be harmful to the global economy.

Consider, for example, devaluation, liberalization, and export promotion—the classic ingredients of the Structural Adjustment Programmes (SAPs) which are imposed on the LDCs as the panacea for their economic woes. Far from stimulating world development, these policies have become a major obstacle, to the extent that LDCs now increasingly feel that the World Bank/IMF SAPs are more part of the problem than part of the solution.

Take devaluation, for instance. According to Chossudovsky, "The short-term gains from devaluation are invariably wiped out when *competing* Third World countries are forced to devalue (in *similar agreements* with the IMF)" (my emphasis). The lesson is simple: devaluation for one country may be fine, but not if all countries are forced to devalue at once. You do not have to be a genius to see this.

The same is true of export promotion. Mihevc points out that "the deliberate promotion of primary exports by the LDCs *as a whole* has led to a glut in the world market for these commodities and the subsequent depression of prices and development for *each LDC individually*" (my emphasis). It is again the same elementary point

The developing countries know, from experience, that their economic salvation lies neither with the IMF nor with the World Bank. Indeed, many believe they would do well to sever their links altogether with these Bretton Woods giants, as now constituted. Presently, being a member of the IMF is like having a noose around one's neck. The noose can be tightened or loosened at will by those who control it, namely, the Western powers. Short of a complete break, there is no way the developing countries can escape the IMF trap.

It would therefore seem imperative for the LDCs to cut themselves off from the IMF and the World Bank, and to do so, not singly, as that would be suicidal, but collectively. This 'shock therapy' might be sufficient to shake the Bretton Woods giants and the entire Western world to the core. After the initial panic, some attempted punitive action, and a little soul-searching, they are bound to come to their senses. A sudden and dramatic withdrawal, if made in concert by all the LDCs, would be nothing short of revolutionary, with far-reaching consequences for the economic and political fortunes of the world at large. It could well be that this is exactly the kind of treatment which the world needs at this particular juncture.

Some have suggested the creation within the developing countries of simple replicas of the Bretton Woods institutions, but I doubt if this is necessary. The already existing financial institutions, including the regional development banks, if suitably reformed, are perfectly adequate for the job (provided they sever their link with, and subservience to, what is left of the World Bank and the IMF). There is no need for further institutional proliferation.

The approach suggested here reminds one of the history of trade unions. One of the earliest lessons of the industrial revolution and the growth of capitalism was the fact that workers had to unite and organize to protect their interests, before they could negotiate a decent wage with their employers. No worker individually could possibly have done this without risking immediate dismissal by his employer. And, in the absence of trade union action, that is, collective bargaining backed by the threat of strike action, nothing could have prevented an employer from paying his workers a bare subsistence wage and getting away with it.

There is a close parallel between this trade union scenario and the perceived need for collective action by the developing countries vis a vis the donor community led by the Bretton Woods giants. No developing country individually can hope to influence the World Bank or the IMF to come to its assistance except on their own terms; terms which are often harsh and ruthless, and clearly intended to further their own agenda. Collective action alone is the answer.

The LDCs' collective strategy should be total withdrawal (or a credible threat of it) from the World Bank and the IMF. These anachronistic institutions have long outlived their usefulness and must be re-moulded from scratch. What they need is not minor cosmetic reform, but a complete overhaul. Their basic Articles have to be re-negotiated afresh.

Granted, it will be a hard nut to crack. The Articles of the Bretton Woods institutions enable them to use—and to be used by—the powerful industrialized countries to defend the *status quo*, in which they have a strong vested interest. Even assuming that all the LDCs could act in unison—itself a tall order—they would still not be able overhaul them, as long as the one-dollar-one-vote principle remains intact. That is why this author is convinced that reform within the existing structure is simply out of the question and that sooner or later a revolution is inevitable.

Essay # 5
GLOBALIZATION AND THE EROSION OF NATIONAL SOVEREIGNTY

With the advent of globalization, and its rapid acceleration, one aspect after another of national sovereignty is increasingly being eroded. In many cases, it is an open question whether the economic benefit of globalization is worth the political <u>price</u>. This is the substance of an ongoing debate, one which is bound to continue, and probably intensify, as the twenty-first century unfolds.

A cursory look at a few of these aspects will suffice to illustrate the point. Probably the most obvious is the manner in which the information "super highway", epitomized by the electronic media and satellite technology, has revolutionized telecommunications, rendering it impossible for any government—least of all the governments of the LDCs—to control the transfer of resources across national frontiers.

Until recently, central banks such as the Bank of England, the U.S. Federal Reserve Bank (and their opposite numbers in other countries) were strong pillars of national sovereignty. This was so because each of them had the ability to control the national currency, foreign exchange and domestic credit, in addition to its supervisory role over the commercial banks and other financial institutions. In that capacity, the central bank had the unfettered ability to regulate the economy, and to formulate and implement fiscal and monetary policy, using such instruments as interest rates, exchange rates and money creation. Governments could therefore exercise national sovereignty by instructing their finance ministers and central bank governors to formulate and enforce economic policy in the manner desired by the government of the day.

But all this is no more. "In both developing and developed countries", says Chossudovsky, "monetary policy no longer exists as a means of state intervention: it belongs largely to the realm of private banking". The same point has been openly acknowledged by leaders of the Seven leading industrialized countries which, in a recent statement, affirmed: "Money creation, including the command over real resources, is controlled almost exclusively by private financiers".

Gone too is the freedom of countries to fix the value of their national currencies. Not long ago, this freedom was at the core of national sovereignty and an important symbol of national pride. It was protected and guaranteed by the central bank's control over the creation as well as the purchase and sale of the national currency in exchange for foreign currencies; plus the control of currency movement into and out of the national territory.

However, with the coming of liberalization, this aspect of national sovereignty has been eroded too. It has been surrendered, not to foreign governments, which would have been bad enough, but to private profit-seekers—the financial speculators—which is, frankly, appalling! As John Naisbitt says, countries do not decide the value of their currency any more: this is done by some 22,000 currency dealers with their computer screens.

Worse still, all this activity happens in a most de-stabilizing manner, due to the volatility of modern high-tech banking, where transactions are carried out around the world and around the clock at the push of a button. The financial speculator's sole aim is to make a "quick killing" on the stock market. This has led some people to suggest that there is need to devise a kind of "financial disarmament" scheme to constrain such de-stabilizing activities.

All this clearly demonstrates that the market liberalization policies being forced on the LDCs by the Bretton Woods giants exact a heavy economic and political toll on those countries. Currencies tumble through massive devaluations. In the ensuing turmoil, heads roll and governments crumble. World Bank loyalists lightly dismiss this as the necessary price for pursuing 'sound' policies. To them, the entire phenomenon is transitory. They euphemize it as 'short-term pain for long-term gain', as the birth pangs of a new and prosperous future. The LDCs, they say, must make 'hard choices', boldly and heroically; tighten their belts, bite the bullet'. Such are the familiar slogans purposely coined to hide the truth behind what are called 'austerity programmes': these are the stock phrases which litter the IMF and World Bank literature, and punctuate the public utterances of their 'experts'.

It should also be remembered that unfettered liberalization is an invitation to money laundering. Even the liberally inclined UNDP admits that the precipitous removal of currency controls before a proper regulatory agency has been established, is a perfect condition for money laundering.

The forced liberalization of the LDC economies also increases unemployment, particularly of unskilled labour. It therefore serves to create a large pool of cheap labour attractive to foreign private investors. Characterized by high-wage economies, developed countries naturally support liberalization in the LDCs because it makes it profitable for them to shift and re-locate their capital where cheap labour is. That is perfectly logical and rational.

Unfortunately, here again some asymmetry is manifest. Whereas the industrialized countries, backed by the Bretton Woods giants, are vocal about the necessity to enforce liberalization in the LDCs, they are mute when it comes to enforcing it in their own countries. The economics is simple: in the LDCs labour is cheap relative to capital, while in the industrialized countries capital is cheap relative to labour. Just as the developed countries find it profitable to re-locate their cheap capital in the LDCs, so the LDCs would find it profitable to re-locate their cheap labour in the developed countries. Thus, the argument for liberalizing capital transfers to the developing countries has logically the same economic rationale as the argument for liberalizing labour transfers to the developed countries.

But look at the real world, and what do you see? Led by the United States, with the tacit connivance of the Bretton Woods giants, the industrialized countries protect their labour markets by erecting all types of immigration barriers in order to ensure that no unskilled or even semiskilled labour from the LDCs enters those countries. This is one more example of the unscrupulous use of double standards for their own selfish ends.

Incidentally, the same countries are quite willing to allow capital and skilled (though not unskilled) labour from the LDCs to go in freely, which says something of their human values. Would it not be interesting to imagine what the world would look like if labour, both skilled and unskilled, were allowed to move freely across international boundaries and re-locate anywhere as easily as capital does? After all, that is what liberalization logically requires. I venture to say that this would have a vastly greater, and more equitable, impact on the development of the LDCs than all external loans and grants combined. It would be the first time that the world had development co-operation in the true sense of the word.

To sum up: liberalization implies the free mobility of resources—i.e. goods and services, as well as factors of production. Whatever hampers such mobility is against liberalization and 'distorts' the proper functioning of a market economy. In orthodox economic literature, spuriously used as the rationale for the policies of the WTO, the Bretton Woods giants, and the industrialized countries, a lot is made of such 'distortions', particularly in decrying various controls or interventionist policies such as price fixing, or state ownership and management of enterprises by LDC governments.

It is claimed that such distortions cause inefficiencies in the allocation and utilization of resources as well as in the distribution of income. Yet it is well known that in no country or economic sector is there perfect mobility of economic resources. Apart from some naturally fixed or immovable assets—i.e. land, buildings and fixed plant—there are various degrees of immobility and various types of natural and artificial barriers to the free movement of economic resources, commonly referred to generically as tariff or non-tariff barriers.

To single out the LDCs for vilification, or to discriminate between capital and labour when discussing market 'distortions' attributable to the immobility of economic resources, is to leave a lot of truth unspoken.

Essay # 6
'INTELLECTUAL PROPERTY' AS A BARRIER TO 'GOOD' GLOBALIZATION

Of all the factors of production, knowledge (commonly styled 'the state of the arts') is of paramount importance. 'Intellectual property' is but knowledge or know-how by another name. It is *new* knowledge which, for the time being, is (or is seeking to be) monopolized and protected for the private benefit of certain individuals; knowledge that is deliberately sheltered from the general public, and regarded as the private property of those who 'produced' it. The high-sounding phrase 'intellectual property' was coined by vested interests as a ploy to give legitimacy to the otherwise obnoxious idea of being selfish or anti-social.

Knowledge is universal and knows no bounds. It is global, or ought to be globalized, in the common interest of humanity. Knowledge and know-how have been growing in volume, complexity and sophistication, in step with advances in science and technology. One of the assumptions of perfect economic competition is the existence of perfect knowledge among competitors. The idea of perfect knowledge does not imply, of course, that perfection has been reached and that nothing more remains to be learned. All it means is that *existing* knowledge is *perfectly shared*; that whatever is known to one is known to all. Thus, no economic agent has secret knowledge or a monopoly of knowledge which could give him unfair advantage over his competitors; there are no production, processing or marketing secrets known to one person which are not equally well known and available to everyone else. In other words, the 'state of the arts' is the same for all.

Under the dual assumption of perfect knowledge and perfect mobility of resources, a competitive market on attaining equilibrium will earn only *normal* profit, since a lower level of profit would drive it out of business while a higher level would attract new entrants into the industry and eliminate the excess profit. It is for this reason that perfect competition is applauded both for its productive efficiency and for its low cost to consumers.

Now, there is no grosser violation of perfect competition—or of 'good' globalization—than an 'intellectual property' regime. The fact that staunch advocates of the free market are also the most ardent defenders of intellectual property only goes to show that the free market theory is honoured more in the breach than in the observance, and those who purport to defend it do so only for selfish motives. In the real world, not only does every economic competitor strive to have a monopoly of knowledge, but laws do exist which protect intellectual property, treating new knowledge as if it was the preserve of a private individual or firm. In this way, knowledge—the most vital productive resource in the modern world—is denied to all but a tiny minority of producers, who are allowed to privatize it as their own personal property. This legal protection confers on them, for years on end, the sole right to exploit their knowledge in producing the good or service in question, in whatever form and quantity, and sold at whatever price, as happen to be most profitable to them, to the exclusion (and often at the expense) of all other competitors.

The intellectual property law is therefore another glaring example of hypocrisy and double standards, tolerated only because it protects the vested interests of the powerful. Granting monopoly rights to an 'inventor' is tantamount to denying a university professor the right to teach—or a university student the right to learn—the latest knowledge in his field. As far as the wider community is concerned, the protection of intellectual property is tantamount to depriving society of the welfare benefits that would have accrued through the full and immediate application of the 'state of the arts'.

While it may be impossible to make a precise calculation, I venture to guess that the total welfare loss to humanity due to the protection of intellectual property has been phenomenal, while the total welfare benefit to the few individuals who have enjoyed such protection must, by comparison, be puny. The proponents of a market-based economy who are never tired of singing the praises of the free market, know perfectly well that knowledge is probably the worst of all monopolies. It deserves to be condemned on the same grounds of allocative inefficiency and social injustice as any other form of monopoly. Calling it by another name does not change that fact.

Let us for a moment play the devil's advocate: what do the defenders of intellectual property have to say? Their argument runs something like this: scientific inventions or technological break-throughs, they say, are often the result of long and expensive research, popularly known as 'R and D' (i.e. research and development). Patents are both necessary and desirable in order to protect their holders and enable them to enjoy a monopoly of their product for a period long enough to recoup their 'R and D' expenses and make adequate profit. They conclude that theirs is a fair and just compensation. Without it, they say, the spirit of enterprise and innovation would be dampened, development would suffer, and the world would be the poorer for it.

Plausible as it may sound, this argument does not, in fact, hold water. To begin with, even if we were to accept it at face value, the granting of monopoly rights would not be the only, much less the best, way to reward an inventor. There surely must be a better way. It ought to be possible to reward a deserving inventor, without at the same time penalizing the rest of mankind by depriving it, for years on end, of the benefits of the invention.

Assume, for the sake of argument, that there is a justifiable case for such a reward. The aim then should be to reward the inventor, *once and for all,* directly and adequately. The reward may take any desired form—e.g. a financial award; or/and a prestigious inscription or citation (like is done for Nobel laureates, Oscar awards, the Guinness Book of Records, or membership of various 'Halls of Fame'). Whatever form it may take, the bottom line is to agree on a formula that provides for a *once-for-all pay-off* that at once does justice to the inventor, and sets free his invention for immediate use for the benefit of humanity.

It is not hard to understand why a once-for-all award is infinitely superior to the present practice of granting (or seeking) an 'intellectual property' monopoly. For one thing, to monopolize knowledge or know-how is to hold up further progress. Knowledge is cumulative. There are times such as the present era of digital technology and satellite communications when new knowledge and its applications are accelerating at a dizzying pace. The potential for development that this knowledge revolution offers in the twenty-first century is truly mind-boggling. The question is: must the world stand still, or mark time, waiting for those at the cutting edge of technology to enjoy their 'intellectual property', when pressing global problems, including disease, hunger and illiteracy, which afflict billions of people could have been contained or solved through the unfettered application of the monopolized knowledge?

To sum up: the granting of once-for-all rewards, rather than monopoly rights, to deserving inventors is to be recommended on the grounds that it would be conducive to open competition and to greater and continued acceleration in the development of science and technology. This is because it would eliminate the unduly long, and certainly unnecessary, time lag or waiting period during which newly acquired knowledge would have been protected as the secret preserve of one or a few privileged individuals. The very elimination of the time lag would, in itself, make it possible for new knowledge to accumulate faster, in the welfare interests of *humanity at large.*

Finally, it should be noted, in passing, that most modern inventions are not the result of the inspired genius of a single individual, but the collective outcome of years of deliberate application by large teams of research scientists. (This unique phenomenon puts developing countries at a peculiar disadvantage due to their lack of adequate resources to invest in R and D). These teams of research scientists work full-time for governments, universities, and corporations on a specific agenda. Any original inventions which their effort may generate, therefore, become the 'intellectual property', not of the individuals themselves, but of the institutions for which they work.

For this reason, institutions which are in the business of R and D may rightly be regarded as agents of development *par excellence*. As such, they are society's trustees or custodians, not the private owners, of any new inventions or discoveries to which their work may give rise.

Being cumulative, new knowledge builds on old knowledge, and new inventions on old inventions. Nothing starts from scratch; it is not as if the wheel is re-invented over and over again. Think of knowledge as a living tree, planted by none other than God Himself. From time immemorial, the tree has been growing, spreading its branches, deepening its roots, and multiplying its seeds. It is a tree which is at least as old as humanity itself; planted, so to speak, on the day that man began to think. At any point in time, contemporary knowledge is the sum-total of the experience of mankind of all generations, past and present. It is truly part of the *common heritage* of mankind. No one has the right to appropriate it to himself; or to conceal or destroy it for selfish ends. Conceivably, such behaviour could be construed as a crime against humanity.

We should take a leaf from the experience and wisdom of the ancient philosophers who maintained that knowledge is universal, and that its universality is something to be scrupulously guarded in those academies of higher learning and research which they appropriately named *universities*. The privatization of knowledge in the guise of 'intellectual property' is an aberration, something of which our generation ought to be ashamed, not proud. It is a manifestation of human meanness, born of the same ignoble spirit that once tolerated kings living in castles while their subjects lived in hovels; or that today still tolerates the co-existence on the same planet of extreme wealth with extreme poverty, a world in which millions of people die because they eat too well, while many more millions die because they have nothing to eat!

Essay # 7
GLOBALIZATION'S HIDDEN AGENDA: A CHALLENGE TO AMERICA'S LEADERSHIP

We may now piece together the various threads of our discussion in order to expose the *unspoken truth* about globalization. It does not require much imagination to see that in propagating and imposing on the LDCs the policies they have—a market-based economy, globalization, liberalization, SAPs, unfettered TNC activity, etc.—and propagating and imposing them in a lob-sided way, the developed countries, led by the United States, have one grand objective in common, namely, world domination, politically, economically, and culturally. *This is globalization's hidden agenda.*

Of course, the United States and the rest will be quick to deny it, at least in public. That is to be expected. Unfortunately, their behaviour cannot be explained in any other terms: certainly not in terms of the high moral profile which they like to portray in the name of democracy, human rights, and poverty eradication. In the final analysis, it is nothing but the base human instincts—*the lust for power and the greed for profits*—that fuel their ambition for global domination. Any appearance to the contrary is deceitful and hypocritical, since everybody knows that what they preach to others is far from what they practice themselves.

To illustrate, consider democracy, human rights, and good governance. Today, no words are used—and misused—more frequently than these. Much development assistance, multilateral as well as bilateral, has become conditional on the observance of democracy, human rights, and good governance on the part of the recipient countries, according to the donors' chosen definition of these terms. Yet, even if it were possible to agree on a common definition, and to accept that these attributes were desirable in their own right and therefore deserved to be respected and upheld, the big question would still remain: is it proper or efficacious to make them preconditions for the granting of financial loans?

This author believes that granting or withholding a financial loan should have nothing to do with rewarding democracy, or punishing its absence, and exactly the same goes for human rights and good governance. Quite irrespective of how those attributes are defined, they are simply not the proper 'tools' for the job.

Or look at it another way. Does the fact that the Bretton Woods giants have money to lend qualify them to judge whether a prospective borrower nation is governed democratically or not? As a matter of fact, of all multilateral organizations, the World Bank and the IMF themselves are probably the least democratic. Based on the one-dollar-one-vote principle, their voting procedures alone leave a lot to be desired. It is not social or economic considerations, much less morality or human compassion, but simply budgetary share, that seems to be the determining factor. How can institutions that are themselves so blatantly undemocratic have the arrogance to preach democracy to nation states?

Alternatively, consider a typical bilateral donor, such as the United States, and see who its major aid recipients are—or have been—in recent years. American assistance to Africa during the Cold War went, naturally, to regimes that were anti-Communist, never mind how corrupt or undemocratic they were—witness Mobutu's Zaire, and Haile Selassie's Ethiopia. Since then, Israel and Egypt have been the main U.S. aid beneficiaries, not because those two countries are the model of democracy, but because it has been in America's strategic interests to support them.

There is no need to multiply examples. The plain fact is that no donor, multilateral or bilateral, merely by virtue of being a donor, automatically qualifies or can arrogate to itself the right to judge or oversee democracy on the part of a potential borrower. It is idle to pretend that foreign assistance is, or has ever been, governed by democratic norms.

For that matter, how democratic is the United States itself? Many Americans admit, at least in private, that the United States is nowadays governed, *de facto*, by big corporations and powerful money syndicates. Ask any U.S. president or congressman and he will tell you—if he is honest—that he could not have been elected, and cannot survive in office, without the financial backing from big business. It makes no difference what the innocuous little voter in the city suburbs says or does: the real electorate, the only one that counts, consists of the big corporations and the well orchestrated, and tightly controlled, party conference.

Thus, in American politics, the electoral campaign manager and the Party fund-raiser are the two most important 'democratic elements' in the electoral process. Indeed, it is no great exaggeration to say that the American people themselves have been sidelined or, in effect, disenfranchised. There are many registered voters who no longer bother to vote, seeing that whichever way they cast their ballots makes no difference. While ordinary Americans may quietly resent this, they have learned to bow to the inevitable, having been brainwashed for centuries into believing that theirs is the best democracy in the world.

Anyone who attends an international conference at which this subject is discussed cannot but wonder: *who* appointed the United States government to sit in judgement over other world governments, and *what is it* that uniquely qualifies it to judge their democracy?

As with democracy, so with human rights and good governance. There is no automatic link between being a human rights observer or violator, and being an aid donor or recipient. Being a donor or recipient is one thing, and being a human rights observer or violator is quite another. There is nothing—literally nothing—that qualifies a potential donor to judge a potential recipient's human rights (or good governance) record.

In principle, then, it is clearly presumptuous, if not ludicrous, to make the observance of human rights or good governance a *condition* for granting or withholding financial loans. What is worse, we know from experience that whenever a loan or other needed assistance has been denied to a human rights violator, it is more often the victim rather than the perpetrator of the violation who suffers the consequences. This has been amply demonstrated every time that sanctions have been imposed on an offend-ing regime, such as Iraq or Yugoslavia today, or apartheid South Africa of yester-year. The unintended result of such sanctions has always been to punish innocent civilians, including women and children, while the real culprits—the dictators and the racists of the day—go scot-free.

Finally, a word on human rights and, specifically, on America's posture in that connection. The fact that the observance of human rights is loudly acclaimed by the United States as a loan or aid conditionality for Third World countries must be viewed with open cynicism. Its irrelevance apart, the question to be answered is: does America itself have the high moral standing needed to assume leadership in the highly sensitive field of human rights?

The Universal Declaration of Human Rights, among other conven-tions, spells out exactly what constitutes human rights. The question is whether, when measured against this yardstick, the United States is fit to judge others on human rights.

The pro-democracy demonstration which the Chinese government ruthlessly crushed at Tiennamen Square in 1990, has been vehemently and rightly condemned by the United States as a violation of human rights. But, is it anything when compared with the decades-old scourge of killings and maimings of thousands of innocent civilians wrought by Jonas Savimbi in Angola, without America ever lifting a finger?

Furthermore, for a country which likes to be regarded as the world's policeman, and the world's human rights torch-bearer, one would have expected the United States itself to set an example by being the first—and certainly *not the last*—to ratify international human rights conventions. But, alas, take a look at the record:

. For 40 years now, the U.S. has failed to ratify the International Con-vention on Economic, Social and Cultural Rights adopted in 1966 by 141 states;

. For 27 years now, the U.S. has failed to ratify the Convention on the Elimination of all forms of Discrimination Against Women adopted in 1979 by 163 states;

. For 17 years now, the U.S. has failed to ratify the Convention on the Rights of the Child adopted in 1989 by 191 states, and already ratified *by all other states.*

Are women's rights not human rights? Are children's rights not human rights? Why should the United States sit on the fence for years on end without ratifying these basic human rights conventions when practically everyone else has already done so? Can one possibly turn a blind eye on such a poor track record on the part of a country which purports to be a human rights watch dog?

Moreover, how can anyone be impressed by a United States which is constantly pointing an accusing finger at China, Cuba, and other Third World countries, while deliberately glossing over Western Europe? Is the United States not aware of the hundreds of thousands of female slaves who are shipped regularly to Western Europe for sexual exploitation? It has been estimated that about 500,000 women and girls from developing and transition economies are entrapped in this slave trade each year—an inconceivable violation of human rights!

Much the same could be said of child labour. To be a credible champion of human rights—and this includes, of course, children's rights—the United States must take, and indeed ought already to have taken, appropriate action against (mostly American) TNCs which are notorious for exploiting child labour. Analysis of international trading chains indicates that for every two G-8 households one child is working under age, often in poor conditions, to serve them. Against such revelations, all the pious talk about labour standards in the LDCs aired by the American delegation at the WTO meeting in Seattle rings hollow and hypocritical.

The Challenge to American Leadership.

In the post-Cold War era, the United States has emerged as the unchallenged monolithic super-power, uniquely placed to assume global leadership. But true leadership depends primarily on acceptance by others. It is something earned, not imposed; based on respect, not fear; on moral principle, not muscle flexing. True leadership is leadership by example, where what you do, or leave undone—rather than just what you say—becomes the real measure of your ability, will, and sincerity. If actions speak louder than words, then America has failed this test.

What President Bush (Senior) once said of the United States Congress can indeed be said of the United States itself. "Congress", he said, "must either lead, follow, or get out of the way!". At present, America is neither a global leader nor follower; it is simply standing in the way. See how reluctantly and belatedly the U.S. pays its United Nations dues. See how it will *not* ratify international human rights conventions, ten, twenty, or even thirty years after practically everyone else has done so. See the way its Official Development Assistance, far from approaching the internationally agreed target of 0.7 percent of Gross Domestic Product, has slid back to its current all-time low of 0.2 percent. Notice its hypocritical double standards on practically every issue concerning trade and international relations, such as food and agriculture subsidies, 'intellectual property', anti-dumping, labour standards, etc.

Mark how fervently the United States supports WTO and the Bretton Woods giants which advance its own interests, and how lukewarm and obstructionist it is towards organizations in which the LDCs have a comparatively greater voice, such as the United Nations General Assembly, UNCTAD, UNESCO, or the UN Centre for Transnational Corporations (which it has since killed). Last but not least, watch its insistence on the blanket imposition of SAPs throughout the developing world, in theory in order to eradicate poverty, but in reality in order to open up markets for trade and investment for the (predominantly American) TNCs. We could go on and on, but need we say more?

To sum up: if the United States expects to be taken seriously, and to assume its rightful role as world economic leader and human rights torch bearer, it must begin by searching its own soul. It should—in thought, word and deed—go beyond its selfish national interests, think global, and temper the use of its political, economic, military and technological power with a sense of humility and justice towards the rest of the world. Above all, before it can exercise effective moral leadership, the United States must rise, *and be seen to have risen,* above the hypocrisy and double standards that so vitiate its image in the world today.

Essay # 8
TOWARDS BALANCED GLOBALIZATION: A ROLE FOR THE UNITED NATIONS

In these essays, we have defined globalization as 'good' or desirable, if it is the kind that promotes or sustains global welfare. Opposed to it is 'bad' or undesirable globalization, the kind that promotes the welfare of particular sectional interests (be it a country, group of countries, or some specific vested interests) often to the exclusion or at the expense of others.

If there is any moral to our discussion, it is this: *there is nothing intrinsically good or bad about globalization.* Moreover, while balanced globalization is in principle attainable, there is nothing inherent in the globalization process to make it balanced. Balanced globalization will not happen by default. It must be deliberately engineered and consciously pursued as a matter of policy.

Unfortunately, we know as much from historical experience as from introspection that nobody, and certainly no government, possesses the required degree of altruism to spearhead globalization towards the desired global balance. Both at the individual and at the national level, human selfishness may well be the worst obstacle the world has to overcome in pursuing this noble goal. We have already seen that even the world leader, the United States, has clearly failed to rise to this noble challenge.

There are two good reasons why globalization needs to be controlled and 'balanced'. The first is in order to ensure that full advantage is taken of good globalization, which must not be compromised or confounded with bad. The second is to forestall a possible backlash which could easily result from bad globalization, if left unchecked. A pertinent reminder is the nineteenth-century British-led trans-Atlantic 'globalization' which, before realizing its full potential, came to a premature end, precisely because of a backlash from those who stood to lose by it. We must heed this lesson of history if the same thing is not to happen again.

Our objective, therefore, ought to be to keep bad globalization at bay, while good globalization is carefully fostered and nurtured. That way, we shall avoid throwing away the baby with the bath water.

These considerations suggest the need for a global authority, which is capable of rising above the narrow selfish interests of individual nations, or group of nations, and promoting world development; a global authority which at once commands international respect, and has the means to enforce its decisions.

Naturally, the United Nations springs to mind. For all its faults, the United Nations is still the nearest thing to World Government, and is probably the only body potentially capable of playing such a role. However, to be effective, it must undergo some radical reforms, of the kind that will render it more democratic, more powerful and better respected internationally than it is at present. The current indiscipline within the Organization—underscored by the overriding self-interest of the big powers and their misuse of the veto—must be ended, in order to make room for a genuinely democratic, just and humane United Nations, that takes into account the interests of all its peoples, rich and poor, young and old, regardless of race, gender, religion or nationality.

Clearly, not every institutional entity that presently bears the United Nations emblem or passes as part of the United Nations *system* can be relied upon to advance the cause of balanced globalization. Organizations like the WTO and the Bretton Woods giants are, for reasons already stated, more likely to hinder than to help the cause of balanced globalization. As now constituted, these institutions, along with certain United Nations organs such as the Security Council, are effectively under the thumb of the big powers, whose interests they tend to protect. They cannot, therefore, be expected to advance balanced globalization in any real sense. Indeed, the complete overhaul of such institutions has to be an integral part of the reform of the United Nations that seems necessary if the Organization is ever to fulfil this new global mandate.

THE END.

ABOUT THE AUTHOR

Peter Eliezer Temu graduated in 1974 from the Food Research Institute of Stanford University, California, with a PhD in the economics of agricultural marketing. A national of Tanzania, Dr. Temu spent his first ten years (1963–1973) in teaching and research: in Kenya, as economics tutor at the College of Social Studies, and later as Research Fellow at the Institute of Development Studies, University of Nairobi; and in Tanzania, as Director of the Economic Research Bureau, University of Dar es Salaam.

From 1974–1977 he served as National Planning Controller in the Tanzanian Ministry of Finance and Planning, and later as Director of the Institute of Finance Management in Dar es Salaam.

For over 19 years, from 1977 until his retirement in 1996, Dr. Temu worked for the United Nations as a professional economist, at various duty stations; devoting half the time to the United Nations Economic Commission for Africa (in Addis Ababa and Lusaka), and half to the United Nations World Food Council (in Rome and New York).

SUGGESTED READING

1. The Challenge to the South: Report of The South Commission, (Oxford University Press, 1990)

2. Chossudovsky, Michel, *The Globalization of Poverty: Impacts of IMF and World Bank Reforms,* 1997

3. Friedman, Thomas, L., *The World is Flat: A Brief History of the Twenty-first Century* (Farrar, Straus and Giroux, 2005)

4. Ghai, Dharam, (Ed.), *The IMF and The South: The Social Impact of Crisis and Adjustment* (United Nations Research Institute for Social Development, 1991)

5. Levitt, Theodre, *The Globalization of Markets* (in Kantrow, A.M. Sunrise …: *Challenging the Myth of Industrial Obsolescence,* John Wiley and Sons, 1985)

6. Mihevc, John, *The Market Tells Them So: The World Bank and Economic Fundamentalism in Africa* (ZED Books, 1995)

7. Naisbitt, John, *Global Paradox* (Morrow, 1994)

8. Panic, M. *Globalization and National Economic* Welfare [book]

9. South Centre, *For a Strong and Democratic United Nations: A South Perspective on U.N. Reform* (ZED Books, 1997)

978-0-595-43379-7
0-595-43379-0

Printed in the United States
89010LV00006B/103-420/A